Faceplant

Chronicles of Facebook's
True Tales & Epic Fails

"A must read for all Facebookers!"
— Lamebook.com

Richard N. Shapiro

Faceplant
Chronicles of Facebook'sTrue Tales & Epic Fails
All Rights Reserved
Copyright © 2013 Richard N. Shapiro.
V2.0

Outskirts Press, Inc.
http://www.outskirtspress.com

ISBN: 978-1-4327-9700-3

Library of Congress Control Number 2012917986

Outskirts Press and the "OP" logo are trademarks belonging to Outskirts Press, Inc.

PRINTED IN THE UNITED STATES OF AMERICA

Table of Contents

Acknowledgements

The idea for the book title, "Faceplant," belongs to Emily Mapp Brannon, who described with clarity over lunch one day her view of the social media world of Facebook as one full of booby traps and irresistible impulses. The booby traps seem obsessive compulsive to many Facebook devotees, and my fascination became this first edition of Faceplant. Many thanks to Cassandra Travis for her research, writing and illustrations, and to Patrick Austin and Mary Hall for their fantastic research and editing. Thanks also to Lamebook.com for providing some great faceplant threads.

Introduction: The FACEPLANT in Social Media

Faceplant - Traditional Definition: Act of hitting the ground face first; a term often used by participants in extreme sports; an unintentional result of risky or stupid activity whereby a person becomes fully inverted from the normal upright position while one or more parts of the face impact the ground simultaneously with the full weight of the body.

Faceplant – Social Media Definition: Unintentional or intentional stupid activity occurring within social media that causes one to appear idiotic in front of potentially thousands of people; similar to traditional faceplants, social media faceplants may cause permanent scarring of reputation and/or ego.

Social faceplants occur on a daily or even hourly basis. Whenever someone posts a status update on Facebook or sends a tweet, there is an inherent risk of suffering a social faceplant. Why are social faceplants so prevalent? Because social media, ironically, lacks an essential aspect of interpersonal interaction – social cues. There is no body language or environmental context when you tag someone in a compromising photo or post a status update.

Think about the embarrassment of carrying a piece of toilet paper on your shoe sole through a posh cocktail party. Fortunately, this embarrassing moment may only be seen by a few acquaintances, and soon becomes a memory. Conversely, an embarrassing

Facebook comment or post can be seen by hundreds, or even thousands, of people, including relatives and close friends.

Oh, and let's not forget that you can remove that embarrassing piece of toilet paper from your shoe and no one is the wiser; a brief moment of humiliation that can be forgotten in a matter of minutes. A social faceplant is very different, and can be much worse. An embarrassing status update or photo can become embedded in cyberspace. Some Facebook posts and tweets may go viral and grab the attention of national media. The posts and tweets we selected entered the cyber-world public domain (we edited and used poetic license on many of them) and represent evidence that once you enter the realm of social media, your faceplant may live on in infamy.

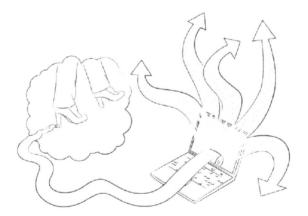

Chapter 1 – Big Mystaque at Work

Song: "Workin' for the weekend" ~ Loverboy

Quote: *"In a hierarchy, every employee tends to rise to his level of incompetence."* ~ Dr. Laurence J. Peter

 Ben: Mystique should not be serving booze to all these minors

36 minutes ago

 Angela: Huuuuuuuge mystaque

34 minutes ago

 Emily: Ah. Greed.

27 minutes ago

Matt: Wow Ben, speaking of "mystaques"…..let me get this straight. While at work tonight you decided it would be a good idea to log into facebook and post a status badmouthing your place of employment? Last weekend when you didn't show up for your shift because, "Your brother was drunk." I thought it was a bit ridiculous but you've managed to top that. Don't bother coming in next weekend. You're fired.

For the love of God, if your boss can read your status updates, do not post messages about your place of employment. If you wouldn't say it to your boss's face, don't post it on Facebook.

According to a study by an Internet security firm, of companies with 1,000 or more employees, 17 percent report having issues with employee's use of social media. And, 8 percent of those companies report having actually dismissed someone for their behavior on sites like Facebook and LinkedIn.

- 15 percent have disciplined an employee for violating multimedia sharing / posting policies

SMH – Shaking my head

- 13 percent of US companies investigated an exposure event involving mobile or Web-based short message services

- 17 percent disciplined an employee for violating blog or message board policies

Chapter 2 – Mentally Flying Creates Vertigo

Song: "Jet" ~ Paul McCartney & Wings

Quote: *"All is mystery; but he is a slave who will not struggle to penetrate the dark veil."* ~ Benjamin Disraeli

Jessica: Is very confused as to how an aeroplane can fly from the north pole to the south pole without going upside down…
20 minutes ago

Stephanie: Now im confused! X
15 minutes ago

Jessica: I've been confused all night lol! xx
15 minutes ago

CMU – Crack me up

 Little: are you jokeing or do you rally
want me to exsplain
14 minutes ago

 Jessica: No explain…
14 minutes ago

 Jem: really?!
11 minutes ago

 Stephanie: Yes!
10 minutes ago

CWOT – Complete waste of time

Little: because of gravaty pulin you towards the earth meens you can keep flying round and round the earth and neva be up side down coz as long as the bottom of the plain down towards earth

10 minutes ago

Just in case you weren't concerned about the future of humanity already, keep in mind this guy is the smart one of the bunch.

Jem: Jess, we're on the side. We don't fall sideways…

10 minutes ago

Stephanie: feel so stupid right now

10 minutes ago

Really? Right now is when you are finally feeling stupid? Anyone reading this felt stupid as soon as they read the first line! They're feeling even more stupid because they've read this far and are still reading!

Jessica: yeah but then if the plain is in the situation how can it land (technically upside down) because the top of the aeroplane would be facing upside down on the ground?
9 minutes ago

Jessica: No Jem I get that cause you fly around..but how do you get upside down? And Steph : YOU FEEL STUPID? I'm the idiot that put it as my status..haha
8 minutes ago

Little: once agen gravaty meens ther no up side down and in space ther is no up and down
7 minutes ago

Jessica: I don't get it?
7 minutes ago

MSMD – Monkey see, monkey do

Are you now asking someone else if you get it or not?!

Little: just go back to thinking the earth flat and you will be fine
5 minutes ago

Jessica: Well I honestly have lived my life thinking that and i've only just realised…Jeeeze..
4 minutes ago

Jem: Australia isn't upside down.
3 minutes ago

Okay, the girl just admitted she thought the world was flat. It's time to quit trying to explain and chalk it up as a lost cause.

CWYL – Chat with you later

Jessica: IM SO CONFUSED..

3 minutes ago

While Disraeli might have a point in some cases, in this situation the "dark veil" of mystery is more like a cinder block of stupid. For all of our sakes, let's hope this infrequent flyer doesn't become a pilot…or even procreate for that matter. Just thinking of flying is giving her vertigo. Whew…altitude sickness struck early.

DARFC – Ducking and running for cover

Chapter 3 – Fleeting Love, Permanent Tattoos

Song: Never Let You Go ~ Third Eye Blind

Quote: *"Logic, like whiskey, loses its beneficial effect when taken in too large of quantities"*~ Lord Dunsany

Sara:

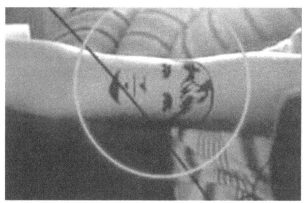

Like · Comment · 20 minutes ago via mobile ·

👍 William ▓▓▓ and 8 others like this.

Hey baby, I wanted to show you in person, but I'm going to be in Calgary a little longer than I expected ☹ but anyways, Surprise!!!! Thanks again so much for paying

EG – Evil grin

for it. The spa was the best valentine's gift a girl could ask for.

Sara

Do you like it?

Like · Comment · 12 hours ago

Bev

OMG! You're soooo devoted! Austin's really lucky to have you Sara. That's so sweet of you. ☺

Like · Comment · 12 hours ago

Sara

Thanks Maria, it hurt but sometimes love can hurt too

Like · Comment · 12 hours ago

EMFBI – Excuse me for butting in

Jenny

Love it, love it, love it!! BTW can I steal that last comment for a status update? Soooo true. Austin, you're a lucky guy. I don't know anyone who would be as devoted as Sara.

Like · Comment · 12 hours ago

Austin

You got my face tattooed on your arm???? What are you insane? You said you wanted a winged tortuous. I designed a winged tortuous and offered to pay for that NOT my face! What the hell were you thinking?

Like · Comment · 12 hours ago

Sara

I was thinking this would be a good way to show you how much I love you. Are you telling me you don't like this?

Like · Comment · 12 hours ago

EWI – emailing while intoxicated

Austin

You don't think a grapefruit sized tattoo of my face, the guy you've been dating for little over a WEEK, on your arm is a little over the top?

Like · Comment · 12 hours ago

Sara

NO! It's supposed to be my present to you! I thought you'd like it! ☺

Like · Comment · 12 hours ago

Bev

I think he's just surprised Sara, he has to like it. It's such a beautiful gesture.

Like · Comment · 12 hours ago

Austin

No I think it's the stupidest thing I've ever seen! What in the world could possibly make me want to see my face tattooed on your arm? What are you branded cattle? Please tell me this isn't

permanent.

Like · Comment · 12 hours ago

LYKYAMY – Love you, kiss you, already miss you

17

Sara

What's that supposed to mean? Are you saying you don't think WE'RE permanent?!

Like · Comment · 11 hours ago

Austin

I think this is a conversation we should be having in private.

Like · Comment · 11 hours ago

Sara

Why? Why are you always trying to cover me up like you're ashamed of me or something? I think everything should be out in the open.

Like · Comment · 11 hours ago

Austin

I think you made that pretty clear when you plastered my face on your bicep. ☺

Like · Comment · 11 hours ago

Sara

I don't understand this, I'm in complete shock. Where is this coming from? Don't you love me?

Like · Comment · 11 hours ago

Austin

Where is this coming from? You post needy comments on my wall daily. Send me the weirdest texts every waking second. Copy my friends contact information from my cell phone and threaten them with it and now this!! I think it's a long time coming. Can we please talk about this on a less public forum?

Like · Comment · 11 hours ago

Sara

Why can't we do this here? It's not like you're going to break up with me.

Like · Comment · 11 hours ago

Austin

Sara, we really need to talk

Like · Comment · 11 hours ago

Girl is about to go crazy in 3.....2......1.....

Sara

Oh my God! You're not actually breaking up with me are you? After all I've done for you? Who is she?

Like · Comment · 11 hours ago

TTTT – To tell the truth

Austin

There's no one else Sara, I just think you deserve someone whose as devoted to you as you are to them. I really hope we can still be friends.

Like · Comment · 11 hours ago

Sara

Can the bullsh*t! Why are you really doing this?

Like · Comment · 11 hours ago

Austin

Really? You're too much. I can't even begin to describe how utterly insane you are. When I say I wish we can still be friends I mean so that my visiting hours won't be as long as family when you're in an institution.

Like · Comment · 10 hours ago

Bev

You don't think that's a little harsh, Austin?

Like · Comment · 10 hours ago

Austin

Harsh? How's telling my friends she knows where they live for harsh?

Like · Comment · 10 hours ago

FBOCD – Facebook obsessive compulsive disorder

Sara

I'm just trying to protect what's mine and understand why you would even consider breaking up with me.

Like · Comment · 10 hours ago

Austin

Well understand this: We're over.

Like · Comment · 10 hours ago

Sara

Well what am I supposed to do now? I've got your face tattooed on my arm!

Like · Comment · 10 hours ago

Austin

I don't know! Give him angry eyebrows or something. You didn't consider this possibility when you were getting it done? I payed for a turtle with wings, when you told the guy you were gonna get my face instead; he didn't give you any warnings?

Like · Comment · 10 hours ago

Jenny

Sara, you know I'm here for you if you want to talk. Forget about Austin, he's clearly the only crazy one here for giving you up.

Like · Comment · 10 hours ago

Sara

Just saw your new relationship status. I guess this is it :(

Like · Comment · 9 hours ago

Sara

http://www.youtube.com?watch?v+rYEDA3JcQqw&ob=av2e

Like · Comment · 9 hours ago

Austin

Not sure Adele is a psychotic megalomaniac, but yeah I get how the situations are comparable

Like · Comment · 9 hours ago

Johnny

Nominate this for the best thread of the year, and really? Adele?? ☺

Like · Comment · 9 hours ago

Sara

Wait. Is this all a joke? Cause if it is, it's not funny.

Like · Comment · 9 hours ago

Austin

I think they are referring to the tattoo. Which to be honest, strains belief. But I'll make this as clear as I can. We are not dating.

Like · Comment · 9 hours ago

Bobby

My children's children will be hearing about this.

Like · Comment · 9 hours ago

Carl

Wow, dude. The second I saw her posts on facebook I knew she was nuts man.

Like · Comment · 9 hours ago

GIWIST – Gee, wish I'd said that

Jenny

She's not "nuts" or a "psychotic megalomaniac!"
Why don't you all just shut up and mind your own
business!

Like · Comment · 9 hours ago

Sara

Thanks Jenny. I think Austin and his so called
friends are showing their true colors

Like · Comment · 9 hours ago

Jean

I want this tattoo on a T-shirt

Like · Comment · 9 hours ago

Jade

I love everything about this

Like · Comment · 9 hours ago

Carl

It's situations like this that remind me of why I'm in
school to become a psychologist…. ☺

Like · Comment · 8 hours ago

RIMJS – Really, I'm just saying

Matt

F-ing Hey Austin, this chick is nuts. That is hilarious. Hahahahaha

Like · Comment · 8 hours ago

Tiffany

Maybe you should make T-shirts with ur face like Joe suggested and give them to the next girl you date….tell them just to wear the shirt rather than get a tattoo.

Like · Comment · 8 hours ago

They say that tattoos are permanent. But in reality, you can over-tattoo a name or symbol if that permanent relationship ends up being not so permanent after all. However, when you have your boyfriend-for-a-week's face tattooed on your arm, post it on Facebook, and subsequently get dumped, that amount of stupidity is pretty hard to erase. Maybe it was just magic marker or a Henna tattoo and the joke is on us after all. The point is it makes you wonder, shake your head in disbelief, and laugh out loud, and that is what a great thread does.

GOL – Giggling out loud

Chapter 4 – Apple Store Faceplant

Song: "No More Mr. Nice Guy" ~ Alice Cooper

Quote: *"If Stupidity got us into this mess, then why can't it get us out?"* ~ Will Rogers (1879-1935)

The Apple Store; table after table of shiny, gloriously fast internet devices: iPhones, iPads and Airbooks. They all call softly to you to touch them, to try them….to log into your Facebook page? Well, some people do. But after you're done updating your status to reflect the food court binges, don't forget to log out, r this may happen to you …

 **Nick I-forgot-to-log-out**: "I like to lick little boy's b@lls and I don't know how to sign out of my FB when I leave the Apple Store!"
Like 1

Oh no, you didn't...

Dad of I-forgot-to-log-out:
"GET OFF MY SON'S FACEBOOK PAGE! I AM CALLING THE APPLE STORE *RIGHT NOW, YOU ARE IN A LOT OF TROUBLE!"*

Wow, turn off the CAPS Lock, Does he really think by typing in all Caps the guy is going to log off?

AAMOF – As a matter of fact

 **Nick I-forgot-to-log-out**: "You don't even know who I am…There are dozens of computers in here, how would the people here even know which one I am on. Don't get pissed because your dumb*ss offspring doesn't know how to log off Facebook. Oh look at that…your son is now interested in men and his favorite activities are fondling scrotum……"

Ok, so yes this is some adolescent's idea of fun. Irritating but easily fixed, simply log onto the son's Facebook account, change the password and erase all the new …err…hobbies. Don't try to win a verbal battle of "wits" with some pimply-faced teenager who is merrily typing away insults.

Dad of I-forgot-to-log-out: "YOU PIECE OF SH*T PUNK! I WILL DRIVE UP THERE AND FIND YOU! THE APPLE STORE CAN TRACE THIS KIND OF STUFF. I AM GOING TO FILE A LAW SUIT SO BIG IT WILL MAKE YOUR HEAD SPIN, NOW GET OFF MY SON'S ACCOUNT!!!"

File a lawsuit against who… your son, the Apple store, the entire mall?? Once again, just go to account settings and change the password. Right now…do it….

Nick I-forgot-to-log-out: "There is no way I am staying in this store long enough for you to get here and from looking at your profile you look like a little b*tch. I'm not surprised that your son is such a retard. Hey! I didn't know your son's religious views were "on my knees to please.""

TBE – Thick between ears

Guess all those threats about lawsuits showed him. Because now he's picking on someone his own size...dear Dad. Ahhh, remember the good old days when disputes over being on one's knees were resolved with a pistol and ten paces?

Dad of I-forgot-to-log-out: "I AM ON HOLD WITH THE APPLE STORE AND MY SON HAS CALLED THE POLICE YOU BETTER RUN AND HIDE! I WILL BE THERE SOON."

Dad's quite handy. He must have an iPhone so he can surf and talk at the same time. But wait, if the son is there, why doesn't he just log on and change the password? Delete all the bad comments, questionable hobbies, and extracurricular activities...

AYSOS – Are you stupid or something?

Nick I-Forgot-to-log-out: "Yeah, that sounds cool but I think I am going to go back into the mall amongst the thousands of other shoppers. Good luck finding me...Tell your son congrats for coming out of the closet. That takes courage. Don't worry, I sent a mass message to all his friends alerting them of his new sexual preferences."

That's just cold.

If someone logs into your Facebook account and leaves unflattering comments because YOU left it open on a public computer, don't freak out. Don't go on a CAPS lock tirade. Take a deep breath, change the password, and delete the offending material. Oh, and you'll look like less of an *ss if you have better written communication skills than the hacker does.

GTK – Good to know

Chapter 5 – No Protection like a Mother's Womb

Song: "Sweet Child O' Mine" ~ Guns N' Roses

Quote: *"Every man must define his identity against his mother. If he does not, he just falls back into her and is swallowed up."* ~ Camille Paglia

These days moms do not just protect their kids from bullies at the bus stop or playground, they protect them even when they grow up and move out, on Facebook, especially when a son's manhood is on the line.

Susan Nozy: Are you gay? I didn't know that, it's impossible to tell from just a facebook post. When you said someone broke your heart, I was thinking she's a b*tch! I guess I was way off!
22 hours ago

MOS – Mom over shoulder

Bryce: wait wut... I AM NOT GAY..NEVA SAID I WUZ..I AM STRAIGHT.. nd yes sum one did break my heart nd yes she is a MAJOR BITCH! I think u have mis read my status wrong Susan..CUZ I AM NOT GAY..NEVA WILL BE..
22 hours ago

That word "and" is entirely too long. Why not just abbreviate it to "nd"? No wonder there is so much sexual preference confusion going on, with all the wuz, cuz, wut, and nd going on.

Diane Ubermom: Yeah Susan my son Bryce is'nt gay he is as straight as they come.
22 hours ago

And in the right corner we have Bryce's mom. Standing at 5'2" this feisty matron likes NASCAR. Watch out...

Bryce: true that Susan..I AM
STRAIGHT AZ THEY COME jus like
my mom jus said

22 hours ago

In this corner we have Bryce, standing at 6'1".
He likes long walks on the beach and enjoys wine
coolers.

Diane Ubermom: yeah so lay off the
gay comments about my son cuz he
is'nt gay Freaking duh. ARE YOU
GAY SUSAN!!!!!RIGHT BACK AT
CHA. How does it feel to get it thrown
back at your face not very good does it.
Ok then quit ask my son Bryce if he is
gay CUZ HE'S NOT GET THE
PICTURE GOOOD I HOPE YOU DO.

22 hours ago

Oh crap, Mom had an hour and a couple of
cocktails and now she's in it for blood. Freaking
duh! Yeah, Susan, are you gay, are you, huh,
huh, huh? It's fairly likely at this point that
Susan has already un-friended Bryce due to his
crazy Facebook stalker mother.

RTH – Release the hounds

Bryce: HEY MOM..No NEED TO BE RUDE TO SUSAN..IT WUZ ONLY A QUESTION..JEEZ..
21 hours ago

Yeah mom, chill. It wuz only a question.

Diane Ubermom: well I'm not being rude im nearly just stating a fact that your not gay that's all if she wants to take it in a wrong way then that's not my problem or my fault cuz its not meant to be in a wrong way.
21 hours ago

Wow, English language denial. Pretty sure there was only one way to take that tirade and it wasn't to a picnic. Once this occurred, Bryce's hopes of a long-term relationship – with either sex – may have been seriously sidetracked (at least with anyone reading this thread). Not many women would accept a monster-in-law like this.

ADIP – Another day in paradise

Having Mom at your graduation is great. Having Mom on Facebook where she can attack your friends…not so great.

Maybe rules need to be established for our parents about crack backs on our "friends" before something confrontational and irreversible happens. Facebook has unlocked the impulsiveness of parents, and they have discovered that with just one click of the mouse they can mortify, embarrass and, in some cases, act just as immature as their children. Bottom line, if Mom demands to be your friend, you may need to set up a fake Facebook account. Just populate it with pretend people and occasionally leave a comment about how much you have been studying, working, or volunteering.

BYKT – But you knew that

Chapter 6 – The Winter of the Stealthy Mosquito

Song: "Streets is Watching" ~ Jay-Z

Quote: *"There is no knowledge that is not power."*
~ Ralph Waldo Emerson

Facebook threads capture a man's logic and reasoning skills in ways no other media can. Case in point:

Osita:
u can practice safe sex, but the streets will kill u

Two hours ago – Like

Michael:
WTF???? How does that make sense??

Two hours ago - Like

Alexis:
?

Two hours ago - Like

RUNTS – Are you nuts?

Osita:
If u really think about it u can protect yoself wen u havin sex but u can't protect yoself in the streets, anything can kill u now a days

Two hours ago - Like

Yes Osita, anything can kill "U" nowadays, like bad grammar, underwear bombers and your fourth grade English teacher.

Michael:
So, That's like saying you can wear a coat to protect yourself from the cold, but you can't stop a mosquito from biting you and giving you AIDS?

Two hours ago - Like

Osita:
1st off bitch, mosquitos are not around in the winter but yea?

Two hours ago - Like

Michael:

LMAO! Hey they can be.

Two hours ago - Like

YY4U – Too wise for you

38

Osita:

Naw nigga dey flie 2 warm places like birds do

Two hours ago - Like

*Migrating mosquitoes heading to the Caribbean are
everywhere, like silly bandz and Zumba lessons. Just one
of the daily dangers modern humans must face.*

Michael:
They go to warm places, right? So what stopping
them from flying into your house and living under a
heater during the winter?

Two hours ago - Like

Osita:
Caus im smarter than you dumb ass 2 be leave my
window open for em 2 get 2 my heater for em 2 bite
me later on.

Two hours ago - Like

*There really is nothing funnier than two people trying to
outwit each other who clearly are short in the wit
department to start with. Even combined these two are
still a beer short of a six pack.*

OTL – Out to lunch

Tenzin:
Lol--leave him alone.

Two hours ago - Like

Osita:
Thank u.

Two hours ago – Like

It's hard to figure out which is worse, the twisted logic behind the connection to AIDS and mosquitos or the challenged typing skills of the authors. Gotta run, need to go check under the heater for the little buggers. In Facebook we trust. Amen.

40

Chapter 7 – Facebook Cheating with "New" Friend

Song: "Lyin' Eyes" ~ Eagles

Quote: *Love is a game in which one always cheats."* ~ Honore de Balzac

Everyone talks about the anonymity of the internet and how sexual perverts and ex-cons can hide behind any profile. Parents warn their kids to never talk to strangers, and warn their teens to never chat with "friends" online that they don't know. Truth and lies are impossible to sort out. Who to believe? Check out this typical yuppie thread…

Ashley: Hey, what's up?

57 minutes ago

Bobby: Hey…what's going on? I accepted your friend request and thought you looked familiar but I can't seem to put a name to the face…help me out here. Have we met before? We should talk on facebook chat.

55 minutes ago

SHMILY – See how much I love you?

Ashley: I thought your profile pic looked cute, so I friended ya ☺ hope that doesn't freak you out! I'm pretty sure we haven't met before. But you look pretty cute in all your pictures. I'd like to chat on fb but the chat thing always freezes up on me or never works right Msg back. Xoxoxoxo
54 minutes ago

Bobby: Haha you're really pretty cute yourself. Really hot actually…..Do you have a boyfriend?

53 minutes ago

Ashley: Noooooooope ☺ It says you are in a relationship though….. ☹

50 minutes ago

Bobby: Oh well, my gf and I are kinda going through a rough time right now. We are about to break up pretty soon anyways so it's not really an issue. How far do you live from DC?
45 minutes ago

LLT – looks like trouble

Ashley: I'm from Baltimore….But why r you guys ending it?

44 minutes ago

Bobby: Nice! That's really close to me.
Uhhh the gf, errrr soon to be ex is kinda crazy. Always moody 24/7 and she never wants to do anything. She is really unhygenic. She takes a shower like ever two-three days and always smells like an old lady because she never uses soap that has fragrences because of her skin allergies.
Soooooo it's not really a big deal. Hey Maybe we should meet up tonight in DC and go to the bars> What do you say?

40 minutes ago

Hmmm, unhygienic and "smells like an old lady"…pretty harsh about his soon to be ex-girlfriend. Maybe his new pursuer will wonder what he will think about her too!

Ashley: Maybe…Do you want to come to my place afterwards for some fun?

38 minutes ago

Bobby: Haha I'm totally down to go to your place afterwards, lol. I'll even pay for the cab. What's your number?

30 minutes ago

YOYO – You're on your own

Ashley: I'll only give it to you if you tell me you're going to give me everything you got tonight when we get back to my place☺

15 minutes ago

Bobby: Dang Ashley! You're getting me all fired up and I want you too! You're hot as hell and I promise you'll get everything and anything you want tonight.

14 minutes ago

Ashley: Good. Because I'm going to F*CKING KILL YOU BILLY. I'M GOING TO F*CKING KILL YOU, YOU SON OF A B*TCH. WHAT THE HELL IS WRONG WITH YOU? YOU F*CKING SICKO. OUR F*CKING RELATIONSHIP IS NO BIG DEAL??????? WE'LL THIS IS NEWS TO ME. WHEN THE HELL DID IT EVER START GOING SOUTH? WHEN THE HELL DID IT BECOME A ROUGH TIME? JUST BECAUSE YOU LITTLE PENCIL PENIS CAN'T GET ANY OTHER P*SSY OTHER THAN MINE. I GUESS YOU WOULD SCREW ANYTHING THAT COMES CRAWLING TOWARDS YOU. LIKE THIS FAKE GIRL. YEA, SHE IS FAKE, ALL HER PICTURES ARE FROM GOOGLE IMAGES, SHE DOESN'T EXIST.

YOU REALLY THOUGHT YOU OUTDID YOURSELF THIS TIME DIDN'T YOU? YOU FREAKING PRICK DON'T EVER CALL ME AGAIN. YOU ARE A WORTHLESS FILTHY PIG. THIS IS THE LAST TIME YOU WILL EVER TALK TO ME. WAY TO THROW 9 MONTHS DOWN THE DRAIN.

Your "NOW" ex gf.

13 minutes ago

Is Facebook flirting cheating? It is if you agree to hang out and hook up. Before you decide you want to cheat on your boyfriend or girlfriend, make sure he or she isn't the one tempting you to greener pastures. Facebook has apparently replaced finding red lipstick on your collar. No telling if that nice looking "new" friend's image is fake or real. No telling if the person who stumbles upon your FB page is even the sex or age they say they are. Let's see, how many CSI or Tru T.V. shows have chronicled murders that arose through "innocent" MySpace, Facebook or twitter acquaintances? You can't count that high. But what about Facebook as the new relationship-wrecker?

VWP – Very well played

One study claimed that twenty percent of divorces involve Facebook. Not convinced? It's so common that there's a website solely dedicated to Facebook cheating: www.FacebookCheating.com. Of course the Facebook tales of woe on that website are countless. The following is a very typical tale shared with the world:

The only reason i didn't want her to have her facebook was because she had around 4,000 friends and about 70% of the friends were males which would try and flirt with her.... We were home alone one night and i got very curious and ...to my surprise [I found] a FAKE FACEBOOK profile my girlfriend had made...Some of the messages were harmless im not gonna lie, but some others were just heart breaking...What bothered me the most...was one of her status updates which reads "I am starting to think that the only true love is the first love the rest are just the ones that help you forget about your first love." I confronted her and asked about the fake facebook and she tells me "its mine and my sister's." I try to believe her and all but i just can't I am currently going out with her because i love her and i can't do anything else but believe her. i don't trust her but i love her.

This one thread sums up the Facebook world so well. Jealousy and envy are two of the prime fossil fuels that provide the energy behind the world of Facebook. How else can one privately spy on the person they should trust the most without leaving their own bedroom?

GWE – Green with envy

Chapter 8 – Fourth Quarter Grand Slams are Rare

Song: "We Are the Champions" ~ Queen

Quote: *"Books had instant replay long before televised sports."* ~ Bert Williams

You know it's fall when:

A. The leaves fall off the trees and collect on the patio
B. Starbucks starts carrying the Pumpkin Spice Latte
C. Your Facebook timeline is filled with a deluge of sports-related updates.

I'm not sure what makes teachers, waitresses and just about every other professional imaginable think that they are professional players/coaches/referees as soon as fall rolls around. But inexplicably everyone who is anyone starts interjecting their opinions and disturbing the "sports-to-actual-information-you-could-use" ratio of your Facebook news feed. That is unless you take matters into your own hands….

CU – cracking up

Michael:
I'm so glad that the Lakers won the super bowl.

About an hour ago

Erin:
What? They weren't playing…

About an hour ago

Ella:
The Lakers are also a basketball team.

About an hour ago

Erin:
I think maybe Michael meant this to be a joke...

About an hour ago

IDGI – I don't get it

Well, clearly even the slightest hint of sports humor has thrown these ladies off kilter. Yes Erin, it is a joke. Perhaps since you are a girl, you don't have 300 armchair quarterbacks clogging up your Facebook newsfeed so you don't quite get the sarcasm.

Gary:
Epic Win/Epic Fail/Epic!

About an hour ago

Michael:
Oh, wait. I meant the Yankees, right?

About an hour ago

Dominic:
Yeah dude, their final home-run was awesome?

About an hour ago

BWTM – But wait, there's more

Michael:
Did you see that hole-in-one that Brad Pitt made in the last inning

About an hour ago

Gary:
Or at the end, when Jeff Gordon caught the snitch?

About an hour ago

Michael:
That was awesome, but my favorite part of the whole game was when Maria Sharapova made that touchdown on 3rd base or when Phil Mickelson did that kick flip into the goal

About an hour ago

PMP – Peeing my pants

Dominic:
I don't know, Tyra Bank's uppercut in the second period really put an end to Libya's defense attempts to prevent the baton from being passed.

About an hour ago

Awesome. They managed to hit every major sport, a couple of made-up ones, and even throw in a Tyra Banks reference to their sport-centric rant. Some days you almost have to hide your entire friend list just so you can get rid of all the sports commentary and get back to the really important stuff...like the newest "Dancing with the Stars" update.

LMAO – Laughing my *ss off

Chapter 9 – Sexual Face-bragging can Backfire

Song: "Don't Stop Believing" ~ Journey

Quote: *"It is better to remain silent and be thought a fool then to open one's mouth and remove all doubt"* ~ *Confucius*

Melanie: My RA just tried to write me up for having sex too loud during quiet hours

36 minutes ago

👍7 *Jason and 3 Others Like This*

Melanie: We f*cked to: "Don't Stop Believing." Most epic sex EVER.

34 minutes ago

James: I wonder if these happened at the same time.

27 minutes ago

Sabrina: You so know your sister can see this…

19 minutes ago

James: And your mom…

18 minutes ago

Bryan: And God

17 minutes ago

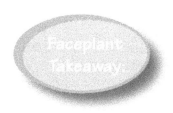

Bragging about your epic sex on Facebook will decrease your future epic sex chances. Women have been faking orgasms for years, but faking sex status updates on Facebook to make a former lover jealous is a new one. Before you start your bragging, you may want to reconsider, because if you think that only your friends are able to see your salacious updates, you're wrong. One study found that posts with sexual references in their titles were "nearly 90% more likely to be shared than average."

NIFOC – Nude in front of computer

Chapter 10 – Weiner-gate: Political Sex Talk

Song: "Promiscuous" ~ Nelly Furtado

Quote: *"Calamity is the perfect glass wherein we truly see and know ourselves."* ~ William Davenant

U.S. Congressman Anthony Weiner enjoyed his role as the lead Democratic "attack dog," not afraid to go after the conservative right's agenda. And he was on a roll, a favorite talking head of many cable TV networks. But let's be frank (pun intended). At some point he got drunk on his own spiked Kool-aid. One day he crossed the line and morphed into a narcissistic caricature that brought his political mojo tumbling down hard and fast. It was supposed to be a private tweet, but oops, he transmitted it to a massive swath of followers instead.

 Weiner: I'm Horny a Lot

Aug 15 at 11:20pm- Like

Yeah, lots of us are, but that's what internet porn's for…or wait…your brand new wife, Rep. Weiner!

JTLYK – Just to let you know

Weiner: whoa. Super intense dream bout u just now.
Woke me up.
Aug 15 at 11:25pm- Like

e-mistress: that is fu*cking awesome! Don't know if you are still up…but we really need to discuss this further! That's the sweetest thing anyone has said to me in a while!
Aug 15 at 11:26pm- Like

Whoa Nelly!! The "sweetest thing" is a powerful politician implying he just had a wet dream with you as the star?

e-mistress: I like these cute new pics of you!
when r you coming to Vegas to help me beat up the right wing crazies?!
September 17 at 4:26pm- Like

What happens in Vegas stays in Vegas. Too bad he never made it there, instead of traveling in cyberspace.

MLAS – My lips are sealed

55

Weiner: this is my "pull my finger" shot. glad you like. I'm ready for a Vegas trip. Truth telling during the day, got a night plan for us?
September 17 at 5:25pm- Like

e-mistress: haha..that was a very loaded question! I've got all kinds of night plans for us! when are you coming?
September 17 at 5:26pm- Like

He probably just did…or…maybe not.

Weiner: dunno. make me an offer I can't refuse.
September 17 at 5:35pm- Like

RU//18 – Are you under 18?

e-mistress: to get us in the mood. first we watch back to back episodes of the daily show and Colbert report...then, to really spice things up we go deface all of my neighbor's Sharon Angle yard signs...then when we are really hot we go to the bookstore and cover all of the Glen Beck books with copies of "The Audacity of Hope!"...I do this about once a week (you can tell I am a very exciting girl!)...or if this I not your thing, we can just get drunk and have mad, passionate sex!
September 17 at 5:38pm- Like

Wow....this e-mistress woman is a true, um...liberal. Maybe she should try running for Congress herself!

Weiner: why choose? with me behind you, can't we both watch daily show?
September 17 at 5:38pm- Like

TMI, TMI! Really, what do you think this is...Animal Planet?

e-mistress: ha-ha! see…you are always thinking! you are so right…aahhh the perfect liberal evening!
September 17 at 6:26pm- Like

Weiner: I hear liberal girls are very, uh, accommodating of others
September 17 at 6:34pm- Like

Yeah, and Congressmen can be real wieners...I mean winners.

e-mistress: of course! it is all about taking care of the little guy!
September 17 at 6:46pm- Like

WDYMBT – What do you mean by that?

58

Weiner: little?! ouch. you'd be surprised how big
September 17 at 6:46pm- Like

Objects in mirror may appear larger than actual size.

Well the whole shebang ended when Weiner twitted… I mean tweeted this picture to the entire world.

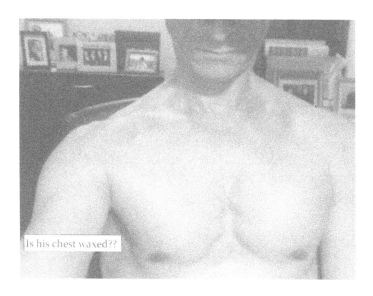

GHM – God help me

It's easy to feel bad for the guy. He got kicked out of office for a cyber-sex scandal that didn't involve any real sex. At least Bill Clinton got the real thing. But don't fret. Porn publisher Larry Flynt – founder of Hustler magazine – made him a "serious" job offer and even vowed to give him a 20 percent raise above the Congressional salary he earned in office. Let's just give the Congressman a period of rehabilitation and redemption. He can host a cable TV news show afterward.

Ok, obviously if you don't want to get caught, don't write it down, video it, type it, e-mail it, twitter it, Facebook it, MySpace it or instant message it. There is no such thing as *private* social media. That's why it's called social! Everything you do leaves little electronic bread crumbs.

Chapter 11 – Babies are Cute; Mucus Plugs are Not

Song: "Baby Hold On" ~ Eddie Money

Quote: *"A baby is a loud noise at one end and no sense of responsibility at the other."*~ Ronald Knox

In the seemingly say-anything world of Facebook, sometimes new mommies-to-be forget to put that little thing called a filter up between their brains and their mouths...or fingers in this case. Don't get us wrong, we want to see your baby pictures, just not the one where the baby is covered in goo and still attached to your umbilical cord. This is a perfect example of when too much information really is too much information!

Beth:
How exciting! Congratulations

About an hour ago

Chantel:
Just lost the mucus plug...won't be long now!

.

Ok. that is one of those things you share with your OB/GYN, not your entire Facebook friend list.

Let's hope Beth is one of the grandmothers-to-be. Even still, yuck. Do sonogram pictures as profile pictures creep you out?

John:
Ohhhh TMI

.

Yes, we agree. Baby belly = cute. Mucus plug = puke.

BNDN – Been nowhere, done nothing

Tiffany:
Oh…….wait….What's a mucus plug?

.

About an hour ago

Ummm…maybe you should ask your mom where babies come from first…

Ok. Ladies, we know you're excited. We also know that you go to one of those baby websites every week just to see exactly what type of fruit (or little person) your little tiny tadpole currently resembles. But for the rest of us who aren't suffering from crippling emotional mood swings, your inner workings may just gross us out. So please, keep it classy mommies.

BPLM – Big person, little mind

Chapter 12 - Cops: You'll Never Catch Us!

Song: "Shooting Star" ~ Smashmouth

Quote: *"The thief is sorry he is to be hanged, not that he is a thief"*~ proverb

So you thought you did some stupid stuff when you were a kid? Maybe you did and maybe you got away with it, but then again you didn't have Facebook to tattle on you. Teens now utilize Facebook to indulge their never ending vanity and self-importance. It seems that every kid age eight and up now has a smart phone. They can tweet, post, and update their way to fame, fortune and now....jail.

It was a pretty good heist for even a professional. Five Pittsburgh teens stole thousands of dollars in cash, boxes of cigarettes, checks and candy. Ok, so maybe professional thieves would have forgone the case of sugar daddies for a sugar momma, but the teens' love of sweets wasn't what did them in.

What did do them in were the photos they posted only an hour after the robbery that featured themselves posing with large amounts of money. Who cares about getting caught? It's obviously more important to let all of your Facebook friends know that you have street cred. Although only "friends" can see most Facebook photos one of the teens had over 200 friends, some of which were adult family members. A few concerned calls later and what do you know? This gang was headed for the slammer. Now if only all crimes could be solved this easily.

If someone robs your home you may be upset, enraged, scared, or all three. But if you are lucky, the perps will quickly post pictures of themselves posing with the heist on Facebook. Fairy tale endings are possible in the world of Facebook.

GRAS – Generally recognized as safe

Chapter 13 - Put Out Or Be Shown Out?

Song: "Good Feeling" ~ Flo Rida

Quote: *"My wife is a sex object - every time I ask for sex, she objects."* ~Les Dawson

 Angelina: Ok…relationship question? If you're dating someone, shouldn't they want to make you feel special and do nice things for you just because it makes them happy to see you happy?? Well nope, this ONE guy I know wants 8-sums, stripper sex and all the perverted stuff in return when he does one nice thing!! SO THAT'S WHY IT'S OVER THIS TIME. I WON'T BE YOUR SKUTT!!!
38 minutes ago

Hmmmm…Skutt? Time to check out the urban dictionary for this one….

> *1. Skutt: (noun) slut and skank combined.*
> *Ex: That b*tch over there is a mad skutt.*

 Jason: Guys date girls for consistent sex. The Vag is powerful, that is why guys normally do things they wouldn't to make their girl happy so in return they can get sex. When I am trying to work I don't want to go to party city so we can decorate the house. I don't want to get a pumpkin and I don't want to go to a haunted house with you because I hate them...I also don't want to get you 4 sexy outfits so you can try them on for me and then NOT F*ck ME! The reason I did all of the above is so I could get sex. The reason any guy does anything for a woman is for SEX. It's sad that I do all that and I still don't get laid. Bottom line....MEN DO THINGS FOR WOMEN SO THEY CAN HAVE SEX. If men did not like sex women would actually have to get jobs and not rely on the fact that they are pretty to get through life!

36 minutes ago

 Angelina: Then pay a stripper, b*tch!!! Don't tell me you love me and base being with me on sex! Find someone else. I already told you.

34 minutes ago

 Chris: You should date a man that would give you the world and not a boy that didn't make you happy!

34 minutes ago

Sean: Chris is trying to get sympathy vag.
31 minutes ago

Jason: When I wake up there is no time. When you wake up HOURS LATER there is no time. When you're bothering me because you're bored and I am working to afford to take you all the places you want to go and buy you drinks so you can get drunk and b*tch for no reason or buying you food when you're hungry, THERE IS TIME. Before we go to sleep at night there is no time.
This is a really fun argument with tons of personal stuff and it's an argument YOU CAN'T win in front of 5,000 people who all agree MEN WANT SEX
30 minutes ago

Angelina: R u stupid? I like sex, but he's perverted and wants it more than a porn star
28 minutes ago

Jeanine: Don't even make me jump back into this conversation…Jason is a douchebag, everyone knows that and Angelina I like you a lot. But I'm sorry you are a dumb*ss for always running back to this *sshole when he treats you like this all the time. Be strong and move on, you deserve better.
25 minutes ago

BLBBLB – Back like bull, brain like bird

Jason: @ Jeanine hot girls like *ssholes…..you wouldn't know that because you're not hot
23 minutes ago

Gonzalo: Men have nice things because women like nice things…If I could f*ck a b*tch in a cardboard box I wouldn't buy a house
22 minutes ago

Wow, that was quite a misogynistic monologue from Jason, but most men seem to agree that men kind of, sort of, well, really do want sex! This is why Facebook was invented, right? Maybe not, but it is terribly hilarious when people hang out their dirty laundry on Facebook for the whole world to see. It makes the rest of us appreciate our lives when we thought our lives were perhaps a little too mundane.

Chapter 14 – First Facebook Contempt Conviction

Song: "I Heard It through the Grapevine" ~ Marvin Gaye

Quote: "*Character is much easier kept than recovered.*"
~ Thomas Paine

Some people consider jury duty an inconvenience and will do anything to avoid it, but it plays a very important part in the American legal system as well as for our friends across the pond, the British (yes, we did get most of the system from the Brits). Facebook is probably the last thing you should be thinking about while on jury duty, but it seems that those wacky Brits love it just as much as Americans. Now we all know that there are some inappropriate ways that Facebook can be used. Here is a list of the top three things you should not use Facebook for:

1. Cyber-stalking exes;
2. Pretending to be a teenager and bullying your kid's classmates;
3. Attempting to sell illegal iguana meat.

Now we have to add a fourth item, contacting the defendant in a court case while you are on the jury, during the trial. Why would a juror put themselves in such a precarious position by chatting with a defendant in the case they are considering?

IANAL – I am not a lawyer

Wealth? Status? Morbid Curiosity? Nope, empathy.

   During a British court case, one of the jurors, a 40-year-old woman, started messaging the defendant on Facebook. She said it was because she empathized with the woman on trial.

Maybe they discussed shoes, shopping, or the outdated hair styles of the judges.

   If only they would have stuck to such frivolities the juror might not be in jail right now. But as the Facebook transcript clearly shows, she grossly violated all the rules of the court by contacting the defendant and even went as far as spilling details of the jury's deliberations:

Sewart: What's happening with the other charge?

Aug 3 at 6:39 pm- Like

Simile: Can't get anyone to go either no one budging pleeeeeese don't say anything. Cause Jamie they could call miss trial and I will get f*cked too

Aug 3 at 6:39 pm- Like

Sewart: I know I have deleted all the messages I wouldn't do that to u don't worry xx

Aug 3 at 6:41 pm- Like

Simile: Don't worry about that charge no way it can stay hung for me lol

Aug 3 at 6:43 pm- Like

Sewart: This is 2nd time in at least ten years all home n dry

Aug 3 at 6:45 pm- Like

Simile: Ha ha ur mad I really appreciate everything. Did u here me say I feel like getting naked? ha-ha

Aug 3 at 6:48 pm- Like

Sewart: Keep in touch and I'll get u a nice present if I get anything out of um. Will find out on Thursday that's when he gets sentenced

Aug 3 at 6:55 pm- Like

Simile: Don't be daft been a pleasure xxx lol

Aug 3 at 6:57 pm- Like

FE – Fatal error

This went on for some time until the defendant told her lawyer, who in turn told the judge. Then all hell broke loose when the court had to dismiss the jurors at a cost the British court said could reach into the millions, including the cost to re-try the entire lengthy case.

Now, because of her faceplant, the juror will be spending some hard time behind bars.

Faceplant Takeaway:

Facebook is great for catching up with old friends, keeping up on friends during our busy lives and checking out pictures of your colleague's wife in a bikini. Facebook is not good for circumventing the instructions of the court. This case just goes to show that just because you delete your Facebook messages, that doesn't mean they are gone forever.

Chapter 15 – "Twilight" Obsession Causes Arrest

Song: "Love Drunk" ~ Boys Like Girls

Quote: *"Harry Potter is about confronting fears, finding inner strength and doing what is right in the face of adversity. Twilight is about how important it is to have a boyfriend."* ~ <u>Stephen King</u>

 Alex: My "friends" are f*ck heads.
38 minutes ago

Rose: ???? Uh oh! What happened?
37 minutes ago

Alex: Long story short. Marc's parents went out of town. I drank too much. When I passed out they all f*cking left me in – front of the police station with a sign that said, "I'm a werewolf, lock me up." Grounded for two months, M.I.C. and community service.
36 minutes ago

Dana: No way!! I'm so sorry Alec that is terrible but sooooo funny! LOL! Werewolf??
35 minutes ago

Marc: We did it because he was talking about how awesome "Twilight" was all f*ckin night
28 minutes ago

PIAB – Payback is a b*tch

The friends get points for creativity. There are no pictures of the incident in question, but one can only imagine him passed out with a sign tied around his neck like a dirty napkin. One thing is for sure, the cops that found him probably laughed so hard they wet their pants.

Facebook should be used solely for the purpose of posting baby pictures, detailing what you ate for dinner and funny YouTube videos. Alright, not really, but you get the picture. Posting something like this could have a less-than-desirable effect on any future scholarships, jobs or even college admissions.

RUS – Are you serious?

Chapter 16 – The Birthday Troll Strikes

Song: "Birthday" ~The Beatles

Quote: *"The best way to cheer yourself up is to cheer somebody else up."*~ Mark Twain

HAGD – Have a great day

Sterling: Happy Birthday dude!

41 minutes ago · Like

Vinnie
its not my birthday...
Unlike · Comment · about an hour ago near Seaford N...

Bryan

Happy Birthday Brother

Like · Comment · about an hour ago

Nick

You were def born on this day...just a great day

Like · Comment · about an hour ago

Jamie

Happy Birthday Kid!

Like · Comment · about an hour ago

Gregg

Happy Birthday

Like · Comment · about an hour ago

R)
Is it sals birthday too

Like · Comment · See Friendship · about an hour ago

👍 Puneet Singh and 2 others like this.

Joey   No just vinces loll

about an hour ago via mobile · Like

Write a comment...

Dick

happy born day guy

Like · Comment · about an hour ago via facebook for BlackBerry ®

Matthew   Was he reborn today or something?

about an hour ago · Like

Write a comment...

OIC – Oh, I see

Tristan:

Happppy birthdaaaaaay my loveeeee<33333

Like · Comment · 2 hours ago

Alex

Happy Fn bday

Like · Comment · 2 hours ago

Rob

Happy birthday big Vinnie v neck

Like · Comment · 2 hours ago

Gerard:

Happy Birthday Vince.

Like · Comment · 2 hours ago

Brooke

Happy Birthday (?)

Like · Comment · 3 hours ago

Melinda
HAPPY BIRTHDAY MAH BROOOOO.
Loves ya   can't wait to celebrate!

Like · Comment · 3 hours ago

TTBOMK – To the best of my knowledge

Meghan
Happy Birthdayyy :)

Like · Comment · 3 hours ago

Patty
Happy birthday my big gay bromo

Like · Comment · 3 hours ago

Jake
Happy bday bra!

Like · Comment · 5 minutes ago

Puneet

I don't know why every one is wishing you
happy birthday when it clearly says July 4th
on your facebook and Sal's as well. I'm not
wishing Sal happy birthday either, for that
matter.

Like · Comment · 7 minutes ago

GIDK – Gee, I don't know

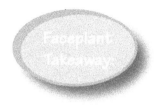

Like the Easter Bunny or Bigfoot, the Birthday Troll is one of the rare fantasy creatures that can appear on your Facebook. However if you are paid a visit by the Birthday troll you can be sure you'll get more birthday wishes than on your real birthday and then your mom will be thoroughly confused…and well, from there things get really crazy.

Though this type of internet prank seems harmless sometimes it can go too far. Take the case of one poor woman from Australia named Kate Miller. When she woke up, got a cup of coffee, and decided to check her birthday party e-vite checklist she found that 10,000, then 30,000, then 50,000 people had RSVPd for a private birthday party event she'd created on Facebook. She had neglected to set the invite to "private." Oops.

Her exact words were:
WTF?????????? WHO ARE YOU PEOPLE? WHY ARE THERE 10,000 PEOPLE WHO HAVE BEEN INVITED??????? THIS IS A PRIVATE PARTY AT OUR APARTMENT."

At 60,000 attendees, she canceled her party. The moral of this story, have fun with the birthday troll but never feed him after midnight or you might end up like Kate Miller.

COBRAS – Come on by right after school

Chapter 17 – The Trailer Park Mollywoppin'

Song: "I'm a Bitch" ~ Alanis Morissette

Quote: *"Speak softly, and carry a big stick."*
~ Theodore Roosevelt

Chris:
Me and Brandon r just chilln hit us up

Three hours ago – Like

Rachel:
Sh*t I tried but u won't answer :/

Three hours ago – Like

Kayla:
Good, he knos better

Three hours ago - Like

TPT – Trailer park trash

Rachel:
Sh*t I tried but u won't answer :/

Three hours ago – Like

Kayla:
Good, he knos better

Three hours ago - Like

Rachel:
F*ck u he's been hitting me up…Sh*t I just stayed wit him Sunday…

Three hours ago - Like

Do you get the impression there is a serious feline fight brewing here?

Kayla:
Haha !! u feel like a big girl now, Maury slut??

Three hours ago - Like

DGTG – Don't go there girlfriend

85

Rachel:
Lmao u dirty man lookin trifling *ss whore i
f*cking mollywop that lil nappy *ss head f urs…sto
talkin sh*t or step up b*tch

Two hours ago - Like

Mollywop: To kick the sh*t out of

Chris:
Stop talkn sh*t on my page an no u didn't…an no
wnt

Two hours ago - Like

Rachel:
U know I did stop lying…and yes the f*ck I will

Two hours ago – Like

Won't what, mollywop or hit you up or do him again?

Kayla:
Wow. I hope u feel grown now lil girl. Grow up a
act CLASSY, ur a f*ckin female….an I believe I tol
you where I lived ONCE already

One hour ago – Like

FYSIGTBABR – Fasten your seatbelts, it's going to be a bumpy
ride

Chris:
Ok stop now u2

Two hours ago – Like

*Oh yes Chris, be a little bit more convincing about
telling these two "ladies" to stop fighting over you.*

Kayla:
Ohh, im deff done. She don't mean sh*t to me and
she DEFFINATLY dont phase me w her
"MOLLYWOPIN" sh*t ma! Ive done told her once
where I lived and its on her frm now she don't want
any just to warn ua, and U kno this! Act Classy no
TRASHY f*ckin slut. An chris…have fun w her
since she stayed w ya n all…NIIIIICCE!!

Two hours ago - Like

Chris:
Txt me

Two hours ago - Like

Which one?? Who should text you?

IJWTK – I just want to know

Rachel:
Yepp he was all up in this so I hope u like the taste [
my p*ssy bitch. And sh*t u r FAR from classy
dirty whore get on somewhere wit ur nasty self. Ar
I will molly wop ur *ss, sh*t ill get outa jail befre
get outa the hospital! Haha so keep stepping C*nt [
come get simple.

Two hours ago – Like

"Come get simple?" I am
still looking through the
urban dictionary definition
for that, but I get her drift.
Not like Rachel is mincing
words here. I'm not sure who
is going to do what to whom. But Chris seems to be
making out like a bandit. Until someone decides to key
his 1978 Ford Pinto which is most likely parked between
the double-wide and various abandoned possessions in
the trailer park. This just makes you want to see a viral
video of one royal mollywopping.

Chapter 18 – Sharing Special Facebook "Coupons"

Song: "You Oughta Know" ~ Alanis Morissette

Quote: *"A man in love is like a clipped coupon. It's time to cash in."* ~ Mae West

 Angela: Mike is 2 cute he got me flowers and some sh*t from bath n body works. And he made me a coupon book! Xoxoxoxo....i love u

36 minutes ago

 Ashley: awwww so sweet, when you getting married already??

34 minutes ago

 Janice: aw! Randy made me a "coupon book" but it was awful. One coupon was a free pass to suck his D@ck, so glad I dumped him. WORST BF EVER!

27 minutes ago

CBB – Can't be bothered

Angela: LOL mike tried 2 sneak 1 of em in there 2. ☺
xoxoxo… maybe I use that coupon tonight????

25 minutes ago

Mike: WTF!!! Why u gotta be tellin everyone about my coupons n sh*t…that coupon book was for u n im gonna take it back if you keep blabbing!!

20 minutes ago

Bob: Hey mike can I get one of them "coupon books" from you? I hear you give a 10% discount on handjobs and you do a sweet buy one get one on a salad tossing!

18 minutes ago

Mike: B*tch, I'll never forgive u for this.

15 minutes ago

LUMTP – Love you more than pie

Kind of like the reprised movie scene of the horny guy with the bucket of popcorn that has a hole in the bottom for his, uh, member, and the desire that the unsuspecting girlfriend will grab a big handful.

This type of special coupon book is not intended to be "shared" in Facebook posts. "B*tch, I'll never forgiv u for this" should be what his "b*tch" parrots back to him for his "special" coupon book.

5FS – Five finger salute

Chapter 19 – Bunny Suit Causes Lawsuit

Song: "Don't Forget to Remember Me" ~ Carrie Underwood

Quote: *"The capacity for friendship is God's way of apologizing for our families."* ~ Jay McInerney

Like · Comment · Yesterday at 4 53pm · ☼

👍 2 people like this.

Dan

Hey, Uncle Tim. Take that crap down.
Like · Comment · 12 hours ago

DBABAI – Don't be a b*tch about it

Uncle Tim

Hah. Make me, this stuff is priceless.☺

Like · Comment · 12 hours ago

Dan

I'm serious. Take the photo down.

Like · Comment · 11 hours ago

Uncle Tim

Awwwww what are you going to do? Are you going to cry about it?

Like · Comment · 11 hours ago

Dan's Wife:

Now boys….

Like · Comment · 11 hours ago

Dan

Shut up and take it down before I take charges out on you.

Like · Comment · 11 hours ago

DEGT – Don't even go there

Uncle Tim

Charges for what? Being an uncle to you?

Like · Comment · 10 hours ago

Dan's Wife:

Surely we can act like adults and agree that since the photo makes Dan uncomfortable that you should take it down. Oh and did you get our Christmas card this year?

Like · Comment · 10 hours ago

Uncle Tim

Danny got his mommy to help him. That Christmas card was awful.

Like · Comment · 10 hours ago

Dan

How dare you bring my wife into this.

Like · Comment · 10 hours ago

Dan's Wife:

If you don't take that photo down I will shove that bunny suit up your *ss.

Like · Comment · 10 hours ago

Uncle Tim

Bring it on, I'm waiting.

Like · Comment · 10 hours ago

Who needs enemies when you have uncles like that? Apparently this guy does. He must have had one heck of a traumatic childhood. Most people would just untag an offending photo and forget about it.

In the ultimate "I'll show you!" Bunnyman sued his uncle for harassment. Unfortunately, posting an unflattering Facebook photo may bring harassment from friends and family but it isn't enough in the eyes of the law to constitute harassment. The case was dismissed. Sure, take the uncle off your friend list, but then,

Bunnyman, get a sense of humor! This was your 15 minutes of fame. You should have licensed the photo, made a few hundred thousand, gotten into a witness protection program, then dropped out of life until things quieted down.

Chapter 20 – Teen Arrested For Ranking Girls' Hotness

Song: "Friends in Low Places" ~ Garth Brooks

Quote: *"Can you imagine a world without men? No crime and lots of happy fat women."* ~ Nicole Hollander

A 17-year-old high school kid ranks girls in his school according to hotness…*What guy hasn't?* But he doesn't stop there. He gives each girl a 5-point ranking based on their physical attributes.

GLG – Good looking girl

At 17, he probably doesn't have the experience or credentials to be making an accurate judgment on the female form, but you have to appreciate his entrepreneurial spirit.

He then added 10-point ranking based on their face and a note whether their "stock" had gone up or down. *Pretty sure his "stock" has been going up.*

However the real ugly part occurred when he gave each girl a derogatory nickname that slammed her for her race, ethnicity and even sexual orientation. Then he made a big mistake and posted his femme fatale list on Facebook. It didn't take long for other hormone-stoked boys to print it out and spread it like a new STD throughout the school. The next thing you know there were a lot of angry dads storming the principal's office. Wow, he was only doing what existing websites do in asking others "hot or not?" Amazingly, the Chicago-area teen was arrested and was charged with misdemeanor disorderly conduct. This is where the First Amendment comes in handy!

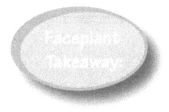

Before the internet super highway of smut, there were, and still are, phone numbers on school bathroom walls. Facebook puts that bathroom wall on a huge billboard for the whole world to see, maybe even encouraging younger men and boys to rank skin-deep attributes of their female counterparts. Wrong... maybe, but criminal? So what happens when some of these numerically indexed nymphs decide to stand up and rank their shallow classmates in a list of their own? Will they drag that sassy school girl down to juvenile jail for raunchy ratings? Probably not. Usually, the First Amendment fully applies to minors. Isn't expressing the "hotness" of teenage girls, or guys, a protected type of expression and speech?

AFAIUI – As far as I understand it

Chapter 21 – Facebook Stink Bomb Detonates on Attorney

Song: "How to Dismantle an Atomic Bomb" ~ U2

Quote: *"Money often costs too much."* ~ Ralph Waldo Emerson

In 2007, a cement truck careened into a young couple's Honda Accord, killing the 25-year-old nursing

student and leaving her husband to mourn her death. He pursued a wrongful death lawsuit in Charlottesville, Virginia against the company and the driver. As the case approached trial there was no question that it was a terrible loss of life and that a major wrongful death verdict against the company would be likely—it was clearly negligent driving. However, several months before trial, the lawyers for the trucking company discovered that the widower husband had posted pictures on his Facebook page allegedly holding a can of beer, wearing a garter belt on his head and an "I love hot moms" T-shirt, along with other pictures, according to court papers. The existence of these pictures truly caused an explosion, especially at the law firm representing him. Many of the facts are public record but this is a fictional conversation between his attorney and the attorney's paralegal:

Husband's attorney: Did you talk to him about his Facebook page?

Paralegal: Yeah, I took a look at it and it's not good. You may not believe this, but he has a picture with a garter belt on his head and an "I love hot moms" T-shirt, taken apparently while partying with friends.

Husband's attorney: You've got to be kidding me! It's taken three years to get this case to a jury. We can't let this wreck all that preparation, trial is only weeks away.

404 – I haven't a clue

Paralegal: I can't believe it either. What are we going to do?

Husband's attorney: Well, they are asking for a download of his entire Facebook page so tell him those pictures better not be there tomorrow.

Paralegal: How could they get access to it?

Husband's attorney: I don't have any idea but it would probably be pretty easy. This **stink bomb** could blow up our whole trial if they get it.

Paralegal: I will get on the phone with him.

Soon thereafter, the husband's attorney sent letters to the trucking company attorney denying that husband had any Facebook page, unaware that the defense attorneys had already captured some of the pages and pictures, despite the attempted deletion of the questionable pictures. In fact, husband's attorney never turned over any such materials and the trial went forward and resulted in a $10.6 million verdict, to be divided in favor of husband and in favor of other family beneficiaries including his deceased wife's parents.

Unfortunately for the husband's attorney and the husband, the court ordered production of all of the emails and files relating to his Facebook page, as well as a subpoena to obtain materials directly from Facebook. In a later court deposition, the husband's attorney called the photo a "stink bomb" that might have caused a continuance, but argued that they were irrelevant.

Just before court hearings about court sanctions, the husband's attorney resigned his license to avoid facing further inquiry. Later, the judge sanctioned the lawyer $540,000.00, the husband $180,000.00, and both sides appealed to the Virginia Supreme Court.

The wrong Facebook pictures can cost parties in lawsuits hundreds of thousands of dollars. However, it seems folks have certain irresistible urges to show one's private affairs to the whole world. Which is worse, a white collar criminal stealing hundreds of thousands of dollars from your bank account or voluntarily parting with those hundreds of thousands of dollars by showing yourself to your Facebook friends in racy photos when you're involved in a major civil case?

IMR – I mean really

Chapter 22 – Duke Graduate's Sexploit PowerPoint goes Viral

Song: "Let's Talk About Sex "~ Salt N Pepa

Quote: *"Nobody will ever win the Battle of the Sexes. There's just too much fraternizing with the enemy."*
~ Henry Kissinger

       Somewhere in between Sex and the City and Chelsea Handler's raunchy book, *My Horizontal Life: A Collection of One-Night Stands*, is the thesis on college copulation by Duke graduate Karen Owen. Karen made all of her 'sexual experiences' into a thesis paper that she developed as a professional-looking PowerPoint presentation.

An education beyond the classroom: excelling in the realm of horizontal academics

Karen F. Owen

Senior Honors Thesis
Duke University

Submitted to the Department of Late-Night Entertainment
in partial fulfillment of the requirements for a
Degree in Tempestuous Frolicking (D.T.F)

May, 2010

LTTIC – Look, the teacher is coming

But this overachiever didn't stop there. In the spirit of Duke academics, she made a PowerPoint presentation with photos of the subject and various charts – very, very interesting charts. She included near-scientific details of the girth, length, and even accent of her, ahem...subjects. Sorry, some of the charts and details are omitted.

Evaluation Process

The Subject's Raw Scores were based on an, admittedly subjective, range of criteria that I had established long before commencing my research project:

- Physical Attractiveness: points were awarded or deducted based on the Subjects' height, body build (muscle mass and definition), jaw-line, quality/texture/cut of hair, facial structure, penile structures, and eyes/eyebrows
- Size: points were determined based on the length and girth of the Subjects' hardware
- Talent: points were awarded or deducted based on how well the Subjects utilized their hands, mouths, and equipment (this category is strictly separate from Size)
- Creativity: points were given if the Subject showed a willingness to go beyond the standard research positions and/or locations (and a knowledge of how to operate once said position was at hand)
- Aggressiveness: points were given if the Subject displayed aggressive behavior and an alpha-male mentality of assuming control of the given situation; points were deducted severely if they simply lay there or did not act assertively.
- Entertainment: points were given for extremely amusing actions, great personalities, quotes, sexts, good senses of humor, or simply dirty talk, and were removed if no noises of enjoyment or talk of any kind was present. In other words, how entertained I was
- Athletic Ability: points were awarded if the Subject regularly performed exceptionally well on the diamond or field
- Bonus: Bonus points were given for extraneous factors, such as the presence of an Australian accent and/or profressional surfing skills. Points were deducted for rudeness or being Canadian.

There's a proud research methods professor out there somewhere...

MIHYAP – May I have your attention please

The issue is not whether the writing is funny, because it is:

> It was on the cab ride back that I discovered he was rude, Canadian, and spoke mostly in French. Needless to say, the warning flags were waving furiously, yet, in the interest of my research and out of a perverse curiosity, I decided to continue towards his apartment...

Or even if she intended it to go viral, because she didn't. She e-mailed it to three of her best friends, one who admitted to forwarding it, and the rest is history. Or should we say "her story."

Would this mischievous memoir have gone viral if it were written by a guy instead of a girl? It probably would have, because of the entertainment value of the story, the witty banter, the self-deprecating humor, and moments of quiet clarity that most modern adults have had or would like to have had in their college exploits.

However, the repercussions probably would have been much harsher on a winsome Romeo than our Jezebel Juliet. Don't blame the Duke lacrosse players or even little Miss Thesis for their kiss and tell attitude.

Blame the wavering line in the sand that separates the politically correct and sexual harassment suits from the movies like "Hall Pass," "Road Trip," and

TMI – Too much information

"Wedding Crashers." Not to mention another favorite: "Good Girls Gone Bad."

Yes honey....what happens in Cabo San Lucas, does not stay in Cabo San Lucas.

It only seems fair after centuries of repression that a woman can look back on a sexual encounter humorously or even, dare we say – brag about it. The problem is that these stories are no longer shared over an appletini with a few close friends, but instead are shared with complete strangers from all over the world.

The virus, it seems, manifests itself in people's inability to not push send or forward.

This story, although extreme, is reflective of how women can now humorously enjoy "hookups" and even brag about them, which used to be considered a strictly male type of activity. But with the growth of social media, spilling the beans about sexual encounters with only your friends is a thing of the past. Leaving us with only two options:

Kiss, tell, and send nude photos to all your friends, who will in turn send it to all their friends, who will in turn post it on www.girlsgonewild.com.

Chapter 23 – Facebook Five Jury: "F*ck the Judge – the Jury's Pimpin'"

Song: "I Fought the Law (and the Law Won)" ~ The Clash

Quote: *"I was married by a judge. I should have asked for a jury."* ~ Groucho Marx

Actions speak louder than words. Well, except for words posted on Facebook by a jury member…after a judge has ordered them to refrain from this conduct.

That's exactly what happened to the infamous "Facebook Five," a group of jurors who deliberated during the criminal trial of Baltimore, Maryland Mayor Sheila Dixon. They ultimately found her guilty of one misdemeanor count of misappropriation of donated gift cards, while acquitting her of some more serious charges. Sheesh…not exactly a high crime.

Fun Fact: A class-one misdemeanor is about the same punishment given for littering (which is oh-so-wrong, by the way.) But probably not any more wrong than what the jury panel members wrote on Facebook. Per a Baltimore newspaper, on New Year's Eve, juror James Chaney wrote:

James: If you see me on the new, remember you don't know me. F*ck the judges and the jury's pimpin'. Bottom line, you don't know me.

Ahhh, the eloquence of modern speech.

James: That message is for the reporters. Y'al know how they can be.

Then two of his fellow jurors chimed in:

Chereese: Yea, yea, do I know.

Elaine: I wish I could feel lonely for a minute – all these peeps on my grill all day long.

WAI – What an idiot

Lonely? How about a little peaceful prison confinement for contempt of court? See how lonely you are then.

Fun Fact: Jury deliberation is a process of thoughtfully weighing options, usually prior to voting. Deliberation emphasizes the use of logic and reason. The Dixon defense team argued the five jurors' Facebook posts during deliberations denied Dixon a fair trial and they sought a new trial.

University of Maryland School of Law professor Doug Colbert said he didn't believe all the talk spelled trouble for the jurors.

> "From a juror's point of view, when you read this letter [from the Judge warning about improper communications] it says, 'I'm asking you not to communicate anymore.'

If Facebooking isn't for communicating, than what is it for?

> It's not saying, 'I'm ordering you or I'm telling you <u>no more</u> Facebook communication,'" he said.

The jurors' response to the hubbub was:

> "Look, we did our job. We made the sacrifice and took three weeks from our homes, jobs, and families. We rendered a verdict; now please leave us alone."

FO – F*ck off

Lawyers now use Facebook to screen jurors, to scope out their likes and dislikes. And it seems jurors use Facebook to discuss trials, even while they are still in progress! This is just another indication that most users don't care much about privacy, as reporters friended the Facebook Five or easily got access to their pages by becoming friends of friends, or friends of the cashier at the grocery store's friend. Maybe jury deliberations should become a reality show including sponsorships in the not-too-distant future. It could ease budget shortfalls and help fund our courts.

JMO – Just my opinion

Chapter 24 – Weed Aint Goin' In Me

Song: "Mama Told Me Not To Come" ~ Three Dog Night

Quote: *"The road to hell is paved with good intentions."* ~ *Karl Marx*

SODDI – Some other dude did it

 Jeffrey: Weed Ain't going in Me! A week ago I was actually offered weed from some dude. He was asking for the exit at the PCC parking lot. I was like ok…the exit is right in front of you. All you need to do is walk straight ahead. After that he was like, "Oh thanks dude."

He then walks forward kind of wobbly and then stops and says, "Hey dude you want to smoke some weed with me?" I was like Oh my goodness I am being offered weed! Of course I have to say no…but if I scream out "NO" he might get up on me or if I lecture him he might like…shank me. I just said "No" as calm as possible.

He bought it and walked away wobbly. That is my experience with saying, "No" to drugs in College. I hope you guys also say no to stuff that can do some harm to your body. Best of luck my friends in high school and those who are going to attend College.

40 minutes ago

 Sally: It ain't going to get in me either, no worries Jeff ☺
37 minutes ago

 Ava: Good for you!
36 minutes ago

SEIYGE – Smoke 'em if you got 'em

Clever: What if you ingest it? Cannabis seeds are used in cooking sometimes.
28 minutes ago

Umm….no they're not. Is he referring to poppy seeds? Or, maybe he is making wry humor?

Tim: Hey one of my suitemate's bro is a dealer…he made our suite smell like weed but he was a cool guy when he wasn't too high.

Another guy I met on the train got kicked out of his house because his parent's found a crap load of weed on him.

Drugs/alcohol is nothing out of the ordinary in college. Get used to it and keep cool underclassman
27 minutes ago

And now the conversation will take a turn for the bizarre courtesy of Tim and his advanced knowledge of drugs and drug dealers.

CAAC – Cool as a cucumber

Jeffrey: Very true Tim! You probably have a greater awareness than me.
26 minutes ago

Tim: @Clever. Chances are you'll know but chances are your drink will be spiked before your food is.
25 minutes ago

Spiked with what...weed? What is he even talking about?

Jeffrey: Isn't it difficult and too much of a hassle to spike the food than the drink
24 minutes ago

Based on that last comment Jeff may need to reevaluate his hopes and dreams of going to college to be a brain surgeon.

HSIK – How should I know?

Does Jeff just lead a very sheltered life or is he fresh out of an Amish community? Only Scarlet O'Hara would ever actually exclaim, "Oh my goodness!"

And what does "getting up on me" actually entail? Take a Xanax, a deep breath, and let's all analyze this situation. The guy asked the college kid to smoke weed with him, not to buy it. It's not as if he pulled a syringe and offered to shoot up heroin.

The "Notes" section of Facebook is probably best utilized by posting real notes...like the directions to your beer pong party or even your communication class survey. On the other hand, such pot-smoking innocence is refreshing in a world inhabited by zombies and werewolf drug dealers.

Chapter 25 – Dad Wins in Cyberspace

Song: "Feels Like the First Time" ~ Foreigner

Quote: *"If a man who cannot count finds a four-leaf clover, is he lucky?"* ~ Stanislaw J. Lec

Justin: Comment when you first met me, how old we were and what u thought!
21 hours ago

Mike 16!
Summer school in HS! Thought u were cool
21 hours ago – Like

Chris
16! 7th Grade Science, Mrs. Morrison!
20 hours ago – Like

DAD ->

Ted
9 months before you were born. I brought you on a date and you left with your mother
20 hours ago – Like

Jenny
I think your dad just won the internet
20 hours ago – Like

DADT – Don't ask, don't tell

117

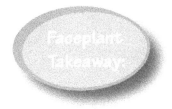

So many times, parents fail miserably in the effort to participate in a thread spun by your friends. How refreshing when a parent hits a home run in cyberspace.

.

GBG – Great big grin

Chapter 26 – FB Format Change Meltdown

Song: "The Times They Are A-Changin'" ~ Bob Dylan

Quote: *"If a small thing has the power to make you angry, does that not indicate something about your size?"*~ Sydney J. Harris

They say if Facebook was a nation it would be the third largest in the world. So when something that large changes something – no matter how small – the masses are bound to complain. Here's just one example of the whining that occurs whenever Facebook changes its appearance or format:

Joe:
What the hell is this "new" facebook? Why can't they leave well enough alone? I almost had that annoying system figured out. Now I need to adapt to more changes. WTH

Aug 15 at 11:25pm- Like

Wonder what happens when something really important changes in this guy's life, like how a Social Security check is printed. This guy is probably terrified of any technology that isn't in the form of a speak n' spell. Of

RTM – Read the manual

course, there are those Facebook acolytes that are ready to do more than complain; they prepare for immediate action.

Greg:
Does anybody know how to delete facebook?
Aug 15 at 11:33pm- Like

Come on Greg, don't be such a drama queen. And anyhow, you know you'll only feel worse in a few days. Your friends will then realize that you have the fortitude of a two-year-old when you reinstate your account.

It's hilarious that people are so appalled that a free service they are in no way obligated to use keeps making changes that mildly inconvenience or annoy them. What happened to the "good ole" America of the 1950s? So easy to never question authority or what the government fed the masses back then. Even earlier, can you believe we fought a war on two fronts, rationed gas and sugar and still did not complain about it? Maybe deleting Facebook will solve all our problems today.

Chapter 27 – Dog-fighting is a Federal Offense

Song: "Walkin' the Dog" ~ Aerosmith

Quote: *"He that won't be counseled can't be helped."* ~ Benjamin Franklin

Sometimes the simplest Facebook post can start a huge sh*t storm of weirdness. Especially when guys have pets as their Facebook icons.

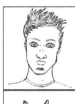

Steve: $45 spent at the drugstore. I better start feeling better soon.

37 minutes ago · Like

Scott: Should of spent it at the, It's Only Natural store. Holistic is the only way to go.

34 minutes ago · Like

DOC – Drug of choice

Jordan: Holistic is a bunch of BS

34 minutes ago· Like

Scott: Lol, that's why all the rich jerks in the world all go to holistic doctors, dumb*ss

33 minutes ago · Like

Jordan: Well I hope you never get sick or you're rich cuz' other than that you might as well kiss your butt good bye

32 minutes ago · Like

Scott: For someone to say something like holistic medicine is BS and have no knowledge of the healing qualities that are contained in all different kinds of plants and herbs is sheer ignorance. Are you going to try and re-elect Obama too?

30 minutes ago · Like

GAHOY – Get a hold of yourself

Steve: It looks like two dogs are arguing on facebook. Just sayin'

29 minutes ago · Like

Steve's comment ended this dogfight! Sweet. Who says pit bulls aren't bully breeds? Only on Facebook could you witness two dogs arguing over the benefits of modern medicine versus holistic healing. Someone call the dogcatcher because these two need to be neutered. (Well they do say it takes away aggression…) Instead of asking their sick friend how he's doing, they're arguing medical treatment options.

IHNO – I have no opinion

Chapter 28 – When to Share and When to Care

Song: "Little Less Talk and a Lot More Action ~ Toby Keith

Quote: *"The basic problem most people have is that they are doing nothing to solve their basic problem* ~ Bob Richardson

We've all had those "friends." Usually they are friends of a friend, and they constantly fill up your newsfeed with complaints and self-loathing. However upon being asked if they are ok by some silly good Samaritan the answer is always the same, "I don't want to talk about it." Well some good advice is…Stop pushing the enter button and sending your woes worldwide!

Karrie Krybaby: Bored..scared..and I don't know what to do.. ☹
I just want this night to be over..
I didn't want to be alone.
I have to work tomorrow too..god I need sleep but can't sleep.
May 15 at 11:25pm

IDGARA – I don't give a rat's *ss

Vinnie: Do you wanna talk about it?
May 15 at 11:25pm

Karrie: no thanks…
this one is a bit personal thank you though
May 15 at 11:26pm

Vinnie: Okay Welcome
May 15 at 11:26pm

Juan: It's ok Kristin. Don't give up.
May 15 at 11:47pm

Isn't "Don't give up" a line in a sappy tune by Peter Gabriel?

HWGA – Here we go again

Jon: I'm deleting you as a friend.
You have the most depressing statuses I've ever read.
 If it's so personal you don't want to talk about it,
don't post it on facebook. Simple as that.
Bye.

May 16 at 12:00am- Unlike 7

When seven of your friends "like" a comment left on your Facebook that describes you as a self-proclaimed attention whore….you may have a problem.

In this world of Kardashian twitter feeds, a few Facebook users have lost the ability to discern a Facebook status update from a personal diary entry. If you don't want to talk about it, you probably shouldn't Facebook about it. Instead, here are some activities you can perform if you can't sleep at night when the urge to enter a status update arises:

1. Clean the bathtub. You probably need to do it anyway, and even if it doesn't help you go to sleep, at least when you wake up in the morning you'll have a really clean tub.

2. Watch old television reruns. This is why Nick at Night was invented! Who doesn't love a little mindless "I Love Lucy?"

3. There's a reason why Angry Birds is currently the top selling iPhone app in almost every country: you can't stop playing it. Start playing Angry Birds and you'll forget what you were dribbling about on Facebook.

Chapter 29 – Tag: Busted by GPS Photo-tagging

Song: "Suddenly I See" ~ K.T. Tunstall

Quote: *"O, what a tangled web we weave;*
When first we practice to deceive!" ~ Sir Walter Scott

Wish you'd get back here!

WYWH – Wish you were here

Facebook has so many convenient features.
Friend-tagging of pictures, location services, etc. You
can tell all your friends what you are doing and where
you are doing it with a touch of a screen! How great is
that?! Not so great all the time, as this scenario proves.

Ahhhh, family reunions. A five-night stay in a
Virgin Islands villa seemed like a good idea when you
bought the Groupon. But once you were elbow-to-elbow
with your sister and her five kids, one of which has just
come down with whooping cough, it strikes you that this
trip might turn out better with a Caribbean queen beside
you at a seaside tiki bar, and fast.

After the various family members drop all the
bags at the Caribbean villa, one large group of childless
family members selflessly volunteers to go to the
grocery store with the only car. How nice! They will do
the key grocery shopping mission for everybody. The
minutes turn into two hours and the baby and toddler
crankiness levels ratchet up to defcon one. But
wait....the phone's ringing. Have they been in a terrible
accident? Did they run out of gas? Were they arrested
by rogue Caribbean cops?

"Sorry sis, but the traffic is killer down here, and
we won't be back for at least another 30 minutes."

Within seconds, the telltale ding of a Facebook
status update echoes across the room from the laptop
computer. Seems that Lil' Sister and the rest of the
missing adult family members are tagged in a photo just
posted to your Facebook page. The group is livin' la
vida loco on the patio of a Caribbean bar with a

NMHJC – Not much here, just chillin'

breathtaking view of the sea, a cold cocktail in hand.

Wow, some faceplanters seem to forget how convenient cell phone technology really is! Location services will update your GPS location even in remote Caribbean locations, and photo tagging is not disabled at island tiki bars.

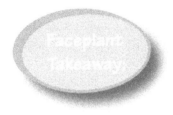

Just like you shouldn't text and drive, you shouldn't let friends tag you in photos at places you aren't supposed to be. No need to ponder "Where's Waldo" when you put your life on the worldwide GPS with locations visited and pictures taken to update your friends, and their friends, and your soon-to-be ex-family members.

Chapter 30 – Southern Comforts Not Comforting

Song: "Southern Man" ~ Neil Young

Quote: *"The very ink with which history is written is merely fluid prejudice."* ~ Mark Twain

Kara

Wall   Info   Photos   B-Day Calendar

Write something...

Attach:

Jordan: a rebel flag on your profile pic? Classy....

12 hours ago · Like

Kara: The babies name is Rebel! Don't need your input!

12 hours ago · Like

Jordan: Even better. Dats the kinda stuff I miss about Missouri. Ha.

12 hours ago · Like

Way to go. Insult a post-partum woman about her profile pic and the name of her baby. You're her "friend" on Facebook because…??

Kara: You bein a smartass?

12 hours ago · Like

Jordan: Absolutely not. I am missin' Missouri a lot lately. The overt racism just isn't here in Omaha

12 hours ago · Like

Kara: I love how idiots pass judgment by a photo! LMAO! That's classic!

12 hours ago · Like

LOU – Laughing over you

Jordan: You have a high school education… if you even did graduate. I have two degrees and a doctorate on the way in a few years. Not to mention your interests include "NASCAR, camping, fishing, hunting and camping." FAIL. Ha-ha

12 hours ago · Like

Kara: And your point is? You can have two degrees and still be a dumb*ss!

12 hours ago · Like

Justin: Hey there is a lot of pride in this family so if you don't like it kiss our rebel *ss's dude.

11 hours ago · Like

Keisha: someone got a problem with my baby's name?

10 hours ago · Like

Kara: Some people like to run their gums when they have no idea what the crap they are talking about.

7 hours ago · Like

Terry: Someone have a problem with my nephew? I think this punk needs to keep his face closed. This family had pride; sorry if this turd has a shallow mind.

7 hours ago · Like

Jason: This jack*ss probably never even stepped foot inside a f-ing college. LMAO. He is probably a high school dropout trying to start sh*t.

6 hours ago · Like

Justin: Well due to the pic it looks like he takes it in the butt by a man, so keep talkin'

5 hours ago · Like

There are two problems with this type of political internet posturing. First, posting your political views and insults on someone's new baby photo is crass to say the least. Second, it will probably convince next to no one that you are smarter, or right. Instead it'll make you look like a jerk, even if your politically correct view of the world may be morally right.

IYSWIM – If you see what I mean

Chapter 31 – Can You Cheat On Yourself?

Song: Your cheatin' heart, will tell on you… ~ Hank
Williams

Quote: *"Mockery is the weapon of those who have no
other."* ~ Hubert Pierlot

Don't you hate it when you're throwing stones at
someone and you don't realize you live in a glass house?

Kallie:
Hate Cheater and anyone who cheats can
rot in hell and im done dating guys with
kids so if u have a kid don't even try to talk
to me!!
22 minutes ago

Ladd:
Karma sucks
21 minutes ago

Kallie:
Ya
19 minutes ago

Ladd:
That was kinda meant for you :\
11 minutes ago

Kallie:
Wtf r u talking about
9 minutes ago

Ladd:
Think about it
9 minutes ago

Kallie:
…..?
8 minutes ago

Ladd:
"Kallie: 'Hate cheaters and anyone who cheats can rot in hell...'"
Remind you of anyone? (other than who this status was meant for*)
6 minutes ago

Kallie:
Nooooooo
6 minutes ago

Ladd:
Ok, let me put this in perspective from my eyes to you:
Kallie, you, hates cheaters and says they can rot in hell.
Kallie and Ladd dated a while back.
Kallie cheated on Ladd with Brigham.
Therefore, Kallie is saying she hates herself and can rot in hell.
And Ladd says Karma is a b*tch.
Understand now? ☺
2 minutes ago

Before damning anyone to eternal purgatory, it may be

best to review your own lifetime of screw-ups. Instead of coming across as tough and in-your-face, this poster ends up looking two-faced and never even realizes it till called out.

OMIK – Open mouth, insert keyboard

Chapter 32 – Grandma Cracks Back on Facebook

"Me So Horny" ~ 2 Live Crew

"Youth comes but once in a lifetime." ~ Henry Wadsworth Longfellow

There are numerous reasons not to friend your relatives, especially those that were around even before television was invented, let alone the internet. First, you can't complain about them without potentially getting caught. Second, you or one of your friends may post something you didn't want the relatives to know about and, well, you may get caught. Third, you may post something that might be offensive to the older crowd, and, all together now, you might get caught.

Natalie: Hey, I don't like this comment. Please remove it.

\---

Comment: Shane (12/15): Me So Horny.

12:11 am

Shayne:
Go to Wal-Mart and buy a sense of humor.

6:21 am

So grandma is up till midnight and the horny guy is up at 6:20 am? Seems kind of backwards.

Natalie:
Go to Wal-Mart and learn some class! Having a sense of humor and being inappropriate are 2 different things! Ask Melilssa how she likes your comment!

11:33 am

Sorry, Grandma. You just lost all credibility when you told someone to go to Wal-Mart to learn some class.

Shayne:
I have alerted the International Internet Police that you are harassing me. Expect them to contact you.

1:02 pm

NBLFY – Nothing but love for you

Natalie:
Harassing? Are you for real? Just because I responded to your comment about me?

4:37 pm

Shayne:
I sent the IIP these most recent comments from you and they will be added to your file. Please answer any calls or emails from Switzerland.

4:48 pm

Unfriend Grandma, and Uncle Wilbur, and Aunt Frances, and anyone else who remembers practicing air raid drills under their desks in grade school. Or, the International Internet Police may intervene.

GM – Good move

Chapter 33 – FB Brings Together Friends & Enemies

Song: "I Will Survive" ~ Donna Summer

Quote: *"There's nothing in the world like the devotion of a married woman. It's a thing no married man knows anything about."* ~ Oscar Wilde

Don't you hate it when Facebook suggests new "friends" for you? It's usually people you haven't friended for a reason. Like the guy you had an office fling with whom you are trying to ignore. Then Facebook in all its glory suggests you "friend" his new wife.

Here's another example where Facebook probably should have kept its "new friend" idea to itself.

LJBF – Let's just be friends

According to court documents, a Washington state corrections officer married his "old" wife in 2001, moved out in 2009, and changed his name in order to remarry without ever divorcing her. "Old" wife noticed he had moved on to "new" wife when Facebook suggested the friendship connection to "new" wife under the "People You May Know" feature.

Wife No. 1 went to wife No. 2's page and saw a picture of her and her husband with a wedding cake," Pierce County Prosecutor Mark Lindquist told AP. He added, "Facebook is now a place where people discover things about each other they end up reporting to law enforcement." Oh, did we mention that a couple years before this, "old" wife was arrested after an altercation with the woman who later became "new" wife?

We can only imagine what the actual Facebook exchange looked like when Facebook suggested that she might want to "friend" the new wife.

FF – Friends forever

Old Wife: Hello. Ok so this may seem a little weird but is your profile picture some kind of gag photo?

54 minutes ago

New Wife: No, of course not. That's one of our best wedding photos.

52 minutes ago

Old Wife: What kind of joke is this? You couldn't have married my husband, you skank.

50 minutes ago

New Wife: Ummm…..who are you, and how dare you put this sh*t on my page? Check the marriage certificate.

48 minutes ago

Old Wife: Yeah. He changed his last name – nice! Why don't you click on some of my pictures and you will see "your" husband with me!

45 minutes ago

New Wife: He divorced you and don't write anything else here either.

44 minutes ago

Old Wife: Think again. Tell your piece of sh*t "husband" he will be hearing from my lawyer soon.

43 minutes ago

New Wife: Don't do that...let me talk to him!

42 minutes ago

Faceplant Takeaway:

Does Facebook ruin marriages? That, of course, depends on the participants. As many as one in five divorce cases mentions Facebook as a primary source of tension, according to the American Academy of Matrimonial Lawyers. In this case, Facebook may result in two divorces, or one divorce and one annulment! The bottom line is it's best to keep your private life private, especially if the people that Facebook thinks you might want to be "friends" with know you in the biblical sense...or if you plan to practice bigamy.

KIT – Keep in touch

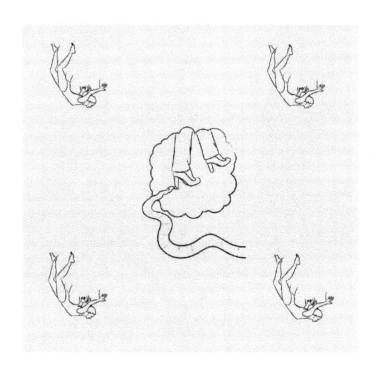

IBF – It's been fun!

www.ingramcontent.com/pod-product-compliance
Lightning Source LLC
Chambersburg PA
CBHW021143070326
40689CB00043B/1085